VISITATIONS FROM GOD

Nancy Dufresne

Visitations From God
ISBN: 978-0-940763-20-3
Copyright © 2004, 2013, 2019, 2024 by Dufresne Ministries

Published by:
Dufresne Ministries Publications
P.O. Box 1010
Murrieta, CA 92564
www.dufresneministries.org

1-5000 2-2500 3-1000 4-1500 5-7500

Unless otherwise indicated, all Scriptural quotations are from the *King James Version* of the Bible.

Scripture quotations marked AMPC are taken from the *Amplified® Bible, Classic Edition (AMPC)*, Copyright © 1954, 1958, 1962, 1964, 1965, 1987 by The Lockman Foundation. Used by permission. www.Lockman.org

The Living Bible copyright © 1971 by Tyndale House Foundation. Used by permission of Tyndale House Publishers Inc., Carol Stream, Illinois 60188. All rights reserved.

Printed in the United States of America. All rights reserved under International Copyright Law. Contents and/or cover may not be reproduced in whole or in part in any form without the express consent of the publisher.

Cover design: Nancy Dufresne & Grant Dufresne

Cover photo: © EB Adventure Photography/shutterstock.com

Nancy Dufresne's photo: © Dufresne Ministries

WORLD HARVEST
BIBLE TRAINING CENTER

M U R R I E T A · C A L I F O R N I A

TRAINING BELIEVERS TO MOVE WITH THE WORD & THE SPIRIT

FOR MORE INFO OR TO SUBMIT AN APPLICATION ONLINE, GO TO

WWW.WHBTC.ORG

OR CONTACT OUR OFFICE AT (951) 696-9258, EXT. 202

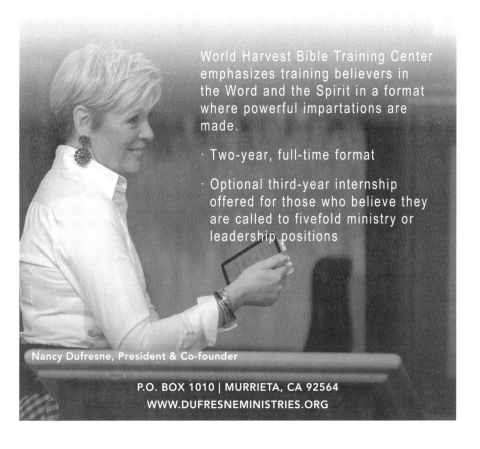

World Harvest Bible Training Center emphasizes training believers in the Word and the Spirit in a format where powerful impartations are made.

- Two-year, full-time format
- Optional third-year internship offered for those who believe they are called to fivefold ministry or leadership positions

Nancy Dufresne, President & Co-founder

P.O. BOX 1010 | MURRIETA, CA 92564
WWW.DUFRESNEMINISTRIES.ORG

Books by Nancy Dufresne

Daily Healing Bread From God's Table

His Presence Shall Be My Dwelling Place

The Healer Divine

Victory in the Name

*There Came a Sound From Heaven:
The Life Story of Dr. Ed Dufresne*

Responding to the Holy Spirit

God: The Revealer of Secrets

A Supernatural Prayer Life

Causes

I Have a Supply

*Fit for the Master's Use:
A Handbook for Raising Godly Children*

A Sound, Disciplined Mind

Knowing Your Measure of Faith

The Greatness of God's Power

Peace: Living Free From Worry

Following the Holy Spirit

*An Apostle of the Anointing:
A Biography of Dr. Ed Dufresne*

Victory Over Grief & Sorrow

Answer It!

The Price of the Double Portion Anointing

Worship

Love: The Great Quest

Books in Spanish

Pan Diario de Sanidad de la Mesa de Dios
(Spanish edition of *Daily Healing Bread*)

Contents

1. Visitations From God 11
2. The Benefits of Having a Shepherd 23
3. Your Role in the Local Church 33
4. Divine Connections 43
5. Guard Against Offense 47
6. Bible Prosperity Is Linked to Your Divine Connection 55
7. Protecting Divine Connections 67
8. Planted in the Local Church 75
9. Perfecting Our Faith 81
10. Keeping a Right Spirit 97

In Closing: Honoring Your Office 101

Prayer of Salvation 103

How To Be Filled With the Holy Spirit 105

Prayer To Receive the Holy Spirit 109

Dedication

I dedicate this book to all the pastors in the Body of Christ who are so vital to the welfare of the sheep. Because of your lives, this earth experiences visitations from God.

Chapter 1

Visitations From God

What is man, that thou art mindful of him? and the son of man, that thou VISITEST him?

– Psalm 8:4

How does God visit man? In the Old Testament, God didn't dwell in His people. When He wanted to visit them, He had to do it in the natural arena, through giving them something to see or feel. As the Israelites traveled through the wilderness, they were able to see a pillar of fire by night and a cloud by day. God's visitations to them were limited to only the physical realm that they could contact with their five physical senses. They had to be able to see or feel something.

But as believers living under the New Covenant, we have God dwelling on the *inside* of us. The believer is to be led by the Spirit of God and not by what is seen in the physical arena. Although God's Kingdom is within us, that doesn't mean that we don't get to experience visitations from God. Yes, God lives in us, but God also *visits* us.

Most of us would think that to have a visitation from God would be to see an angel, to have a vision of Jesus, or to have some other spectacular, spiritual experience. These things would certainly qualify as a visitation, but we can look to the Word of God to see the definition of a visitation.

> **LUKE 19:41 & 44**
> **41 And when he** (Jesus) **was come near, he beheld the city** (Jerusalem)**, and wept over it,**
> **44 ...because thou** (Jerusalem) **knewest not the time of thy VISITATION.**

What was their visitation? A God-filled man in their midst! How many times God stood in the midst of His people, but He was never recognized because they only saw a man and failed to see God in the man! The Bible defines a visitation as a God-filled man sent to the people.

When God moves to visit people, He sends a man – a man filled with God!

People cry out for God to manifest Himself to them and fail to see God's man, their own pastor, who's in their midst.

People are looking for spectacular dealings from God and missing their supernatural visitation from God through their pastor.

Martin Luther was a visitation from God. John Wesley was a visitation from God. Smith Wigglesworth was a visitation from God. Dr. Lester Sumrall was a visitation from God. Billy Graham was a visitation from God. Kenneth E. Hagin was a visitation from God. Ed Dufresne was a visitation from God. When God wants to visit man, He sends a man – a God-filled man! How thankful we are to have been blessed by such visitations from God. Those on the earth have come to know God better because of such men – these visitations from God. We know that God's Spirit resides in us, but thank God for His visitations as well.

At different times of tests, trials, and crisis, every believer has received a visitation from God in the midst of their hardship by having heard a sermon, received a word of encouragement, or read a book from men of God such as these.

But I want you to know that the greatest visitation the believer can receive in their life is the visitation that comes through their own pastor!

Every time your pastor steps in the pulpit, delivers God's Word, and obeys the Spirit of God, you are receiving a visitation from God! Every Sunday morning you have an *appointed* time of visitation! Every scheduled service throughout the week is an appointed time of visitation for you through your pastor.

The apostle, prophet, teacher, and evangelist are sent to minister to the Body of Christ at large, but the pastor is the office that's sent to *you!* No other ministry office can take the place of the pastor in your life.

Many times, Christians cry out to God to speak to them about a particular test they're going through or about a situation they're facing. But were you in church on Sunday?

Were you in church during the mid-week service? God was visiting and speaking to you through your pastor. Were you there to hear what God had to say to you?

Hear Your Answer

If you're facing a financial need and you go to church Sunday morning and your pastor announces that he's going to preach on marriage, don't unhook! Don't think that you won't get your answer to that financial situation. The Holy Spirit is the greatest Teacher you'll ever have. As the pastor preaches on marriage, the Holy Spirit will take his words and teach you what you need to know about your situation.

It's so amazing how the Holy Spirit can take one sermon and answer 500 questions that 500 different congregation members may have.

You have to come to church in faith. You have to come *expecting* God to talk to you! You need to be able to say to your spouse or loved one when you're on the way to church, "When we get to church, God's going to speak to us through our pastor, and we're going to get the answers we need!" As believers, we are to live a life of faith. Faith carries an expectancy with it. Expect God to talk to you through your pastor!

If you were to go out of town for a weekend and had to miss church, you could return the next week and ask a congregation member, "What did pastor preach on last

Sunday?" And he may answer, "Oh, he preached on walking in love." You might ask another church member, "What did pastor preach on last Sunday?" And he may answer, "He preached on walking in your authority." You might walk up to a third congregation member and ask the same question, and the reply might be, "He preached on forgiveness."

Well, who's right? They all are. They all heard according to their need. That's why you should always expect God to talk to you, no matter what the sermon topic is, because the Spirit of God will help you through that sermon according to your need.

Respond to the Spirit

Come to church expecting to hear your answer through your pastor's sermon. Come ready to *respond* to the Spirit of God. My husband made a statement that stuck with me. He said, "The reason people don't receive more in a service is because they don't *respond* more!"

The Bible instructs us to "yield to the Spirit." To "yield" simply means to respond. What you respond to is what you yield to.

We are to respond to what the pastor is teaching or preaching. We're not to sit in church cold and lifeless like an old, dead fish, but we're to respond. Out of the abundance of the heart the mouth will speak. It's not just a quiet, inward heart-felt agreement, but the mouth gets involved when the heart gets full. Say, "Hallelujah! Praise God! That's right, Pastor!" Respond to what is being said, but let it come out of your spirit. It's not mental response, but heart response that makes all the difference in one's life.

If a husband goes to put his arm around his wife's shoulders, but she pulls back from him, her response will cause him to be grieved and pull away. In the same way, when the Spirit starts moving among us, if we fail to respond, we grieve Him, and His anointing will lift. So, we must come to church expecting to receive from Heaven through God's man and ready to play our part in responding to the Word and to what is being taught.

Too often, we expect the pastor to really preach a great sermon and have a "blow-out" good meeting, but did you know that it's not just up to the preacher to have a good meeting? It's up to the congregation also. A congregation can fuel a good service or shut it down by failing to respond to the Spirit of God and by failing to respond to the pastor.

Mark 5 records that Jesus had what we could call an "up" meeting! He went to Jairus' house, and Jairus' daughter was raised from the dead. Now that's an "up" meeting!

Leaving Jairus' house, Jesus went directly to His hometown of Nazareth and had what could be called a "down" meeting. His hometown was offended at Him, and the Bible tells us that *"...he could there do no mighty work"* (Mark 6:5). He went there to teach the Word, heal the sick, and work miracles, but the crowd wouldn't respond right, so people went with their needs unmet.

When people fail to respond in a service, their needs will go unmet, and it won't be the preacher's fault. The congregation has a responsibility toward the success of a meeting. If they fail to respond, they fail to receive! That's why we must come to church in faith – expecting and responding!

Show Up!

But what if people neglect their church attendance? How will they be able to receive what God has for them through their pastor?

Jesus appeared to His disciples after He was raised from the dead and told them to tarry in Jerusalem until they were baptized in the Holy Ghost. Jesus later appeared to a group of 500. But on the day of Pentecost, when the Holy Ghost filled the Upper Room, only 120 were present. Where were the other 380 people? They just didn't make it! They missed the next thing God was doing! They missed one of Heaven's greatest outpourings on planet Earth!

How many times Christians miss an outpouring God had for them just because they fail to show up faithfully for church services! How careless many Christians have become toward appointed times of God's visitations that come through their own pastor.

You Need a Shepherd

Matthew tells us,

> **MATTHEW 9:36**
> **But when he (Jesus) saw the multitudes, he was moved with compassion on them, because they FAINTED, and were SCATTERED abroad, as sheep having no shepherd.**

Notice that without a shepherd, sheep faint and are scattered. The Bible doesn't say without an apostle, a prophet, an evangelist, or a teacher that the sheep faint and are scattered, but it's when they are without a shepherd.

Now, don't misunderstand me. We need all the fivefold offices, for Ephesians tells us,

> **EPHESIANS 4:11-13**
> **11 And he gave some, apostles; and some, prophets; and some, evangelists; and some, pastors and teachers;**
> **12 For the perfecting of the saints, for the work of the ministry, for the edifying of the body of Christ:**
> **13 Till we all come in the unity of the faith, and of the knowledge of the Son of God, unto a perfect man, unto the measure of the stature of the fulness of Christ.**

Thank God for ministers who may come to your city and hold crusades and conferences, but when their meetings come to an end, who's there to continue feeding you God's Word? Your pastor!

No minister is as important in your life as your pastor! He's the one who's there to see after your spiritual welfare on a continual basis. The other four ministry offices are sent to the Body of Christ, but your pastor is sent to *you!* The other four ministry offices are primarily concerned with the Body of Christ at large, but the pastor's primary call is to *you!* He's the one anointed to watch over your soul with the spiritual equipment that belongs to the pastoral office. The apostle, prophet, evangelist, and teacher are primarily offices that will travel, but the pastoral office is the one that always stays local, living among the sheep.

The other fivefold offices are to assist and aid the pastoral office. The other four offices should point the sheep toward the office of the pastor.

Charles Finney, one of the greatest evangelists that we have record of, shook whole cities with his revivals. For one year he stayed in a particular city conducting a revival, and he recorded that 100,000 new converts were added to the local churches through the year-long revival. He only considered as his fruit those who became part of a local church. Finney saw that if his fruit was to remain, it must be brought into a local church. He pointed the sheep to the care of a pastor.

All of the fivefold offices must seek to have the fruit of their ministry increase and build the local church.

Watch Your Diet!

You should feed on the teaching and preaching materials of your own pastor more than you feed on any other minister's materials. You should get hold of your pastor's materials and feed on them, because he's the one anointed to be your primary spiritual supply. All other ministers can be a supplemental supply, but your pastor is to be your primary feeder.

It's a blessing to receive from other ministers, but you need your pastor's materials more than you need anyone else's, for he's anointed to speak into your life in a way no other minister is.

A Safe Diet

When we minister overseas, we always attempt to eat more Americanized food because that's what our digestive systems are used to. We don't try to shock our bodies by eating spices and dishes that would confuse our systems. Yes, their native dishes are food alright, but it's not the same kind of food we're used to. They're prepared and served differently than we normally eat.

Likewise, different ministers prepare and serve up their spiritual food in different ways. Yes, what they're serving may be from the Bible, but it's not all prepared and served up the same way. By eating from too many spiritual plates, you'll confuse your spirit. Your spirit will be confused trying to digest a variety of spiritual foods.

At dinner time, it's not right for you to go to the neighbor's house to eat when Mama has your meal prepared for you at home. Stay home and eat from your own table – you'll be safe eating there! Stay in your own local church and be fed from your own pastor's ministry. Quit visiting every church meeting in the city. You might get food poisoning from some doctrine and mess up your whole spiritual system.

When my mother cooked a holiday meal, it tasted different than anyone else's. Even if someone else made the same dishes my mother made, they still didn't taste the same. There's nothing like Mama's home cooking!

Likewise, there's nothing like eating your pastor's spiritual food! Another minister may preach from the same Bible passage your pastor preaches from, but it won't always taste the same.

Many Christians have created great difficulties for themselves by floating around and getting their spiritual food from just anywhere. They become spiritually unhealthy because they eat from too many different pots of doctrines.

I know which ministers God has put into my life to feed me and to be a supply to me, and I don't go eating from a lot of different ones. When I stay with those God has hooked me up to, I get fed what I need.

Stay Close to Home

An area where some believers fall into danger is when they neglect the services in their own local church while following around a traveling minister. It's perfectly fine to attend the services of a traveling minister, but when he travels on to another city, you shouldn't go with him. He's called to travel, but sheep are called to be faithful to their own church. Believers will confuse their spirits by leaving their pastor to follow around a traveling minister. A traveling minister does not have the equipment needed from God to be your pastor. Stick close to your pastor!

To properly mature the saints, all the fivefold offices listed in Ephesians 4:11-13 are needed, but the office of the pastor is the most needed office, for the pastor stays with the sheep. He's there with them day in and day out, and his presence in their lives keeps them from fainting and from being scattered. The pastor is the one who watches over the souls of those in his sheepfold.

Chapter 2

The Benefits of Having a Shepherd

> *But when he* (Jesus) *saw the multitudes, he was moved with compassion on them, because THEY FAINTED, AND WERE SCATTERED ABROAD, AS SHEEP HAVING NO SHEPHERD.*
>
> – Matthew 9:36

The shepherd, or pastor, is the adhesive force in the lives of the sheep, for his oversight of the sheep keeps their lives from being scattered. He helps hold all of God's blessings in the lives of the sheep; he helps keep those blessings from being scattered out of their lives. If you are submitted to a pastor and Satan attacks you, you have the right to say, "No you don't, Satan. I have a shepherd, and you can't scatter me!"

The shepherd's presence in the lives of the sheep is a strengthening force that keeps the sheep from fainting.

As a Christian, you have a race to run, and no one else can run it for you. But without a shepherd in your life, you will faint along the sidelines and never reach the finish line – never reach the end of what you were born to accomplish. No runner who faints can finish his race. Likewise, without a shepherd you can't finish the race God has called you to run, because you will faint without a shepherd. Yes, you can still go to Heaven, but you will go there without having fulfilled your heavenly assignments.

You can look at a believer's life and know whether or not they have a shepherd. If they are fainting, their lives are void of the only thing that can keep that from happening – a pastor.

Don't Be Scattered

Without the office and anointing of a shepherd in the life of the believer, their life will be scattered – that's what Matthew 9:36 tells us. What does it mean to be scattered?

Sickness is a scattering of health. Without a shepherd in their life, the believer opens the door to sickness.

Let's back up one verse and read:

> **MATTHEW 9:35**
> **And Jesus went about all the cities and villages, teaching in their synagogues, and preaching the gospel of the kingdom, and HEALING every sickness and every disease among the people.**

This is the same multitude for whom Jesus was moved with compassion, the ones without a shepherd. But I want you to see their condition when they came to Jesus – they were sick. Those without a shepherd open the door to sickness.

When you have a pastor called by God, who preaches the whole Gospel, he will teach you how to walk in your authority over sickness and disease, but without a shepherd, you won't be properly taught how to walk in your authority.

Without a shepherd, your family will be scattered. Children won't be serving God; homes will be full of strife and unbelief. Many marriages even end up in divorce courts – a place of scattering. A true pastor will teach you how to walk in love, and if you'll be a doer of the Word you hear, it will bear much peace in your home.

Without a shepherd, your finances will be scattered and lack will dominate. Lack is simply a scattering of provision. But a true pastor will teach you about sowing and reaping, and then God's blessings will abound.

Some people may argue with this, saying, "Well, Jesus is all I need!"

Yes, Jesus is all you need to *redeem* you, but you need all of the fivefold gift ministries, especially that of the pastor, to help you *mature* spiritually. Your new birth could only happen because of Jesus, but your spiritual maturing requires all of the fivefold ministries. To be redeemed is one thing, but to become spiritually mature in Christ is another. Jesus knows you need all the fivefold offices – that's why He gave them. He wouldn't have given them if we didn't need them.

MATTHEW 9:36 (AMPC)
When He saw the throngs, He was moved with pity and sympathy for them, because they

were bewildered (harassed and distressed and dejected and helpless), like sheep without a shepherd.

Notice all the words of failure surrounding the person without a shepherd – bewildered, harassed, distressed, dejected, and helpless. What's their remedy? Submit to a pastor! That's a place of safety.

Hebrews 10:25 reads,

> Not forsaking the assembling of ourselves together, as the manner of some is....

The Living Bible reads,

> Let us not neglect our church meetings, as some people do....

The Amplified Classic Bible reads,

> Not forsaking or neglecting to assemble together [as believers], as is the HABIT of some people, but admonishing (WARNING, urging, and encouraging) one another....

Admonishing, warning, urging, and encouraging people about what? Warning them about the danger of neglecting and failing to be faithful to church attendance. Maybe we should have a warning on the front of every pulpit proclaiming, "WARNING – Failure to attend church services is hazardous to your faith, your health, your marriage, your children, your finances, and your fellowship with God!"

A Good Habit

Notice again what the Amplified Classic translation says, *"Not forsaking or neglecting to assemble together [as believers], as is the HABIT of some people...."*

God created you with an ability to form habits in your life so that you could form right habits that would help shape your everyday life. Right spiritual habits, right mental habits, and right physical habits are imperative to develop in the life of the believer.

Jesus would frequently go to the Mount of Olives to pray; it was a favorite location of His. Luke 22:39 tells us, *"And he came out, and went, AS HE WAS WONT, to the mount of Olives...."* The Amplified Classic Bible says, *"And He came out and went, AS WAS HIS HABIT, to the Mount of Olives...."*

Notice that Jesus created the *habit* of going aside to pray; He developed that spiritual habit.

Many people would assume that Jesus went aside to pray because the Spirit of God led Him to. That may have been the case at times, but this passage of scripture lets us know that He had developed a *habit* of having certain times of prayer, and He prayed because He had a habit that caused Him to give Himself to prayer, to give Himself to fellowshipping with His Father.

Jesus proclaimed, "I only say what I hear My Father say. I only do what I see My Father do." When did He hear His Father? When did He see what His Father was showing Him? No doubt, during those times of prayer in the morning when

He went aside. His habit of prayer put Him in a place where He could hear His Father's words and see His Father's works.

Whether you realize it or not, the habits you have developed in your life are either bringing you into the place of hearing and seeing your Father or drawing you away from hearing and seeing your Father. Whether you realize it or not, every man lives by his habits – good or bad. Your habits shape your life, and your habits cause you to walk with or walk away from God.

If someone begins smoking, their body will get in the habit of needing nicotine. It's the same with alcohol and drug use. If you do those things very long, you'll develop a habit of your body needing them. No, the devil didn't do that. You got your body in the habit of needing those things. Yes, the enemy will energize those habits, but if you will do away with them, then he will have nothing to energize.

We all know that if you continue using cigarettes, alcohol, and drugs, these bad physical habits can kill you prematurely. Now, if bad *physical* habits can kill you, what do you think bad *spiritual* habits will do for you? They can kill you prematurely.

One of the most dangerous, bad spiritual habits anyone can develop is that of neglecting to attend church services.

Let's look again at the habits of Jesus' life.

LUKE 4:16
And he came to Nazareth, where he had been brought up: and, as his CUSTOM was (we could

rightly say, "as his HABIT was"), **he went into the synagogue on the sabbath day....**

Jesus had the habit of being faithful to church attendance. If Jesus, the Son of God, needed to be faithful to church, how much more do we need to be faithful to church? Make your decision to be faithful to church attendance. You can't be like Jesus without it.

Those with this bad habit of neglecting church will try to justify it many times by saying things like, "Well, I'm just too tired," or, "It's too hard to get all the kids up and dressed," or, "That's the only time I have to stay home with my family," or, "It's too far to drive." That kind of thinking, and other thoughts like that, will never excuse their disobedience to the Word. *God* is the One who said to not neglect church services! That's not a suggestion from your pastor; that's a command from God! (*"Not forsaking the assembling of ourselves together..."* Heb. 10:25.) God gives us commands to protect us, not to restrict us.

The majority of people that attend our church in Southern California moved from other locations just to attend our church. That's how important it is.

If there's not a church that teaches the Word in your region, then pray and believe God to raise one up.

Train Up a Child

I grew up in the Methodist church, and there's one thing I'm particularly grateful that my mother instilled into me –

the habit of church attendance. We were there every time the doors opened. We would never think of missing church anymore than we would think of missing school or missing work.

In fact, if you wanted trouble, just be bold enough to whine to my mother, "Do we have to go to church?" If you did, trouble was calling you by name! Church attendance was a law in our house, and if you asked Mother if you had to go to church, then you were trying to break her law – and that meant trouble! No, we just knew, as sure as the sun will rise, we will be going to church!

I'm always amazed at the parents who ask their children if they want to go to church! Those same parents wouldn't think of asking their children if they want to go to school! We must lead our households as Joshua did when he proclaimed, *"As for me and my HOUSE, we WILL serve the Lord"* (Josh. 24:15). Joshua let it be known that he had made that decision for himself and his household, *"...WE WILL serve the Lord."*

Some parents may argue, "Well, if my child doesn't want to be there, they won't get anything out of it." But, again, they wouldn't make that same argument regarding school. A mother wouldn't say to the father, "I don't think little Billy should go to school today. I don't think that he is going to get anything out of it because he doesn't want to be there."

Having your child in church is putting him in the atmosphere where God is speaking and moving. We know that God's not moving in the mall and in the movie theaters the same way He's moving in the church, so get him in church! No, your child may not be glad to be sitting in that service, but he is still sitting under the influence of the Holy Spirit Who is moving in the service, and His influence will have an effect on your child.

As a parent, it is your responsibility to be an example of good spiritual habits to your children, and it's your responsibility to develop the habit of faithful church attendance in your children. No child is born with discipline and good habits – those must be developed – and parents can't expect children to develop the discipline alone. You have to help instill in them right habits by placing demands and expectations on them. But you must also be their example by establishing your own good spiritual habits.

The Bible instructs us to, *"Train up a child in the way he SHOULD go..."* (Prov. 22:6). Don't train them up in the way they *want* to go, but in the way they *should* go. You don't ask them for their permission to be trained. You train them!

Some parent may say, "Well, they've got to make their own decisions sometimes." Yes, when they're trained! If they are continually making wrong decisions, then they're not trained, and you need to be making some decisions for them as you continue to train them.

If you teach a child that it's alright to habitually neglect church attendance so that they can participate in other activities, functions, and sports events, you're giving them a bad spiritual habit. You're teaching them to serve the wrong things. It can cost you much to teach your children that it's alright to put sporting events and other activities above church events on a continual, consistent basis.

You had better make sure that what you're teaching them to serve is big enough to deliver them! Teach them to serve God through being faithful to church. Church services are the highlight of your week. Nothing else is equal to their importance! Teach that to your children.

Chapter 3

Your Role in the Local Church

As we were growing up, not only did we attend all the services, but we served in the church. We would clean or do any kind of work that needed to be done. Most members in our church were active that way.

When I was in the eighth grade, our church organist moved away, and I was about the closest thing in the church to an organist since I took piano lessons. So, the choir director came up to my mother and said, "Would you ask Nancy if she would play the organ for church?" (God bless his brave heart!)

My mother quickly spoke up, "She will be glad to do it!"

The director said to my mother, "Well, we'd like to pay Nancy for doing it."

"Oh, no!" Mother insisted. "She won't take money to serve this church! It's the least she can do for her church."

I'm so grateful that I was taught early in life that money was never to be tied to serving. If a church pays you for doing a service, that's fine, but if you won't serve unless you receive money, then you have a heart problem.

We must teach our kids the habit of church attendance and the habit of serving without expecting pay for it. Teach them how God will reward them instead.

Well, I played that organ in the church from the eighth grade until I graduated from school and moved away to go to college.

However, when I was in the eleventh grade, the music director again approached my mother and stated, "Carolyn, Nancy is here for every service, every choir rehearsal, weddings, and funerals, and we've never paid her anything in the past four years. We'd like to pay her something."

"Okay," Mother relented, "you can pay her $5 a month."

So, I was thankful to get the $5 monthly salary. But that really didn't matter – I would be playing that organ whether I received money or not.

Then, one year later, when I became a senior in high school, the music director again approached my mother and said, "Carolyn, Nancy has a car now and has expenses with that. We would like to pay her more."

"Okay," Mother again relented, "you can pay her $20 a month." So I received that.

No, my mother wouldn't allow the church to pay me much of a salary, but when it came time to go to college, I received a significant amount of scholarship money that was much more than any salary I could have received. God blessed me with scholarships just because I was faithful to serve in our local church.

But the greatest thing I received from being the organist was a habit – a good *spiritual* habit of church attendance and serving, and I'm so thankful for it.

In fact, I have two brothers who have pioneered their own churches and a sister who is active in her local church. How did that happen? Not by chance, but by habit – one good habit of church attendance!

Spouses With Good Church Habits

Parents, when your children become old enough to marry, make sure the ones you allow them to date or to be around are those who also have the habit of church attendance. If your children marry someone who isn't faithful to church attendance, their spouses will pull them out of the church.

These matters are of such great importance to their spiritual lives and future.

Safety in the Local Church

Many Christians have the thinking that says, "You don't have to attend church to be a child of God." No, but you do have to attend church to be an *obedient* child of God! Those who neglect church and are unfaithful in their church attendance are disobedient to the Word of God, and the Bible tells us to warn them of the danger they are putting themselves in (Heb. 10:25, AMPC).

There is safety in the fellowship of the local church and in being united with other believers. Those who are not faithful to a local church are isolating themselves from this safety and are opening themselves and their families up to all kinds of needless attacks. There is safety and protection in unity. I'm reminded of what I heard Dr. Lester Sumrall state, "The banana that leaves the bunch always gets peeled!" Many believers are away from the protection of unity and are open on every side to the devil's attempts to "peel" away the blessings of God from their lives.

As thankful as we are for good books, teaching CDs and DVDs, and faith-filled Christian television broadcasts, they will never take the place of our need for a pastor. These things are able to supplement us in our walk, but they cannot be to us what a pastor and the local church are to be to us.

Taking daily vitamins with our food may be a good supplement, but they could never replace the supply we get from eating healthy, balanced meals. Likewise, to only live on Christian teaching materials and broadcasts is like trying to live off vitamins with no food. Vitamins can't properly work without food, and teaching materials and broadcasts don't properly work in your life without the food of the Word that comes from a pastor.

If you or a family member ended up in the hospital, those ministers who publish the teaching materials and make those religious broadcasts aren't going to come visit you – but the pastor or someone from your local church will. If you face a crisis, those other ministries aren't going to help walk you through that hard time, but your pastor and your local church will.

Some may even argue, "Well, I used to go to a church, but when I faced a trial, no one came to see me!"

Well, were you a faithful, active member? Did you serve and participate in that church? Those who are unfaithful in church attendance won't be missed, even if they are absent because of hardship. Those who slip in at the last minute and sit on the back row, only to slip out as soon as the last prayer is said, don't build fellowship with others there, and they don't become a vital part and supply to that church family, so no one even knows they're facing hardship.

The Bible instructs us in 1 Thessalonians 5:12, *"...know them which labour among you...."* We only get to know those who labor among us – those who don't labor among us don't become known.

What does it mean to "labor" in the local church? It means to serve one another. There are many departments in every church that need workers, so find a department that needs your help and serve there.

Those who put the most into the local church get the most out of it; but those who put little into the local church get little out of it.

The Right Church

Many in the Body of Christ don't understand the seriousness of being under the *right* pastor and being part of the *right* local church.

Where the Word is being taught, you can be fed and grow. The church you'll be fed in is the one that is teaching who you are in Christ, what belongs to you in Christ, faith, healing, Bible prosperity, and how to live a victorious Christian life.

One day, I was talking to a woman who was telling me about her friend who had become ill and died at middle age. The woman had many questions about her friend's death and concluded by saying, "When I get to Heaven, the first question I'm going to ask Jesus is, 'Why did my friend die so young?' "

When she said that, the Spirit of God spoke to me and said, "She doesn't have to wait until she gets to Heaven to find that out. I'll tell her right now. She died prematurely because she attended the wrong church. The church never taught her about divine healing, and when she needed healing, she didn't know how to receive it."

Now, I didn't know this woman's friend, but I told her what God said about it.

It could be life and death what church you attend. If you're taught that God makes you sick, then you'll get sick there. But if they teach you that Jesus is the Healer, you can get healed there – and so can your family.

It's so important that you attend the right church. The right church to attend may not be the one you were raised in. The right church may not be the one closest to your home. The right church may not be the one where your family and friends attend. But the right one will teach the *fullness* of God's Word – not just a portion of it.

God Will Lead You

God will lead you to the right church when you ask Him to. But you must always let Him do the choosing – not you. You don't "find the church of your choice" – you are to follow God's leading. Go where you're fed.

1 CORINTHIANS 12:18
But now hath GOD SET the members every one of them in the body, AS IT HATH PLEASED HIM.

Every believer is set by God within the Body to do their part in the Body of Christ. God has empowered and gifted each one of His children to work, function, and bring a supply to the Body of Christ. You can't do that without belonging to a local church and serving in the local church He directs you to and sets you in. When you bring your supply to the local church He sets you in, it pleases Him.

You please God when you attend the church where He has set you. That's the place where God's blessings and supply will flow into your life to the fullest measure.

Many may say, "Well, I don't know if I'm in the right church," or, "I never actually heard God tell me to attend this church."

Well, just go where you're fed! Do you get spiritually strengthened and nourished where you're attending? Does your faith grow stronger there?

When you follow God's leading on where to attend, then that pastor is anointed to speak into your life, and God anoints you to receive from him. But if *you* do the choosing of where to attend church, that pastor won't have the same supply for your life, and you won't receive all God has for you. God will bless you as much as He can, but it's just far better to go where God leads you because that's where you'll fit; that place will be "home" to you, and God's blessings will flow much richer.

If you see a flock of sheep in a field, you'll not find one among them who chose their shepherd. No, the sheep had no voice in it. The owner of the sheep determines who shepherds the sheep.

Even so, none of us belong to ourselves; we were bought with a price, and we belong to God. God is the One who places the sheep under a shepherd. Jesus is the Great Shepherd, but He entrusts the sheep to those shepherds under Him. How safe we are under the shepherd of *His* choosing!

Ephesians 4:16 tells us that all of us are part of the Body of Christ and that every joint receives a supply from the joint it is connected to.

When a member of the Body is out of joint, not in the place where God has put it, the whole Body suffers. If a joint is out of place with the rest of the Body, it quits receiving its supply from the other joints. If a believer doesn't get connected and stay connected to the local church and pastor that God has placed him with, his supply is cut off. Many believers dry up spiritually when they don't stay connected to the pastor God puts them with because their spiritual supply gets cut off when they get out of joint, or out of place.

This is true not only for the church member, but also for ministers.

Chapter 4

Divine Connections

Every believer needs a pastor. But also, every minister needs a pastor, a spiritual father, to speak into their life. Kenneth E. Hagin was the spiritual father to my husband and me for years. We didn't leave our spiritual father – if we had, we would have gotten out of joint, and our spiritual supply would have been cut off. Our spiritual health and well-being were connected to our spiritual father.

When I married my husband, I was still a baby Christian. I had only been saved and filled with the Spirit for a couple of years. But after we were married, my husband became my mentor. He was my Bible school, and he did more to train me in the Word of God and the moving of the Spirit than anyone else. My spiritual supply was connected to him.

Now, I still have a man of God who is my pastor, for I need a man of God to speak into my life. I travel to be in his services regularly, and I feed on his materials. As I do, God speaks to me – revelation flows into my spirit. He is a supply into my spiritual life, and I protect that divine connection. As I stay connected to him, I continue to receive a supply of the Word and Spirit through him.

I need the continued supply of this divine connection in my life if I am to remain spiritually healthy.

The Spirit of Faith

Many believers and ministers make a tragic mistake in their spiritual life by not realizing that their blessing is always connected to another man. If I were to break my connection with the one God has supplied me with, I would lose a blessing of the Lord on my life, and my life and ministry would be weakened.

These men who have imparted to me all lived under a strong spirit of faith. I want the spirit of faith to permeate my life, so I stay connected to men who have a strong spirit of faith.

Faith is the force of God, the flow of God. We will take our faith to Heaven with us when we leave planet Earth, so we must invest in our faith. I protect my faith by surrounding myself with those of strong faith. I purpose to surround myself with other ministers who live under the spirit of faith. The spirit of faith is fed by meditating and acting on the Word of God and by associating with those who have the spirit of faith.

Paul wrote to Timothy saying,

> **2 TIMOTHY 1:5**
> **When I call to remembrance the unfeigned** (sincere) **faith that is in thee, which dwelt first in**

thy grandmother Lois, and thy mother Eunice; and I am persuaded that in thee also.

Paul shows us that faith is transmitted by those with whom you closely associate.

Well, just as faith can be transmitted, so can unbelief and doubt. So, guard against those things by closely associating with those who have a strong spirit of faith, and it will cause your faith to be strengthened.

Paul stated, *"For I long to see you, that I may IMPART unto you some spiritual gift, to the end ye may be established"* (Rom. 1:11).

I spend thousands of dollars traveling to be in the services of men of strong faith. It's well worth any price I pay to have a spirit of faith and the anointing imparted into me by being in their services. It will help me to run and finish my race.

Some people place more value on money than on the spirit of faith and on the anointing. They would rather save their money and not make such a trip than spend whatever it costs to be associated with men of strong faith.

The first association we must protect is the one we have with God and His Word. John 15:7 tells us, *"If ye abide in me, and my words abide in you, ye shall ask what ye will, and it shall be done unto you."* We must develop the spiritual discipline of feeding on God's Word and fellowshipping with God through prayer. But our next associations we must protect are the ones we have with those men God has brought into our lives.

Pastors, just as sheep need to be faithful to attend church services to receive what they need, you must also be faithful to be around the men God has put in your life to receive what you need. Those are divine connections you must value, honor, and protect so that your life and mantle can be properly nourished.

If you don't stay rightly and tightly connected to those God has joined you to, then you don't receive all you could have received.

Chapter 5

Guard Against Offense

And he went out from thence, and came into his own country; and his disciples follow him.

And when the sabbath day was come, he began to teach in the synagogue: and many hearing him were astonished, saying, From whence hath this man these things? and what wisdom is this which is given unto him, that even such mighty works are wrought by his hands?

Is not this the carpenter, the son of Mary, the brother of James, and Joses, and of Juda, and Simon? and are not his sisters here with us? And they were OFFENDED at him.

But Jesus, said unto them, A prophet is not WITHOUT HONOUR, but in his own country, and among his own kin, and in his own house.

And he could there do no mighty work, save that he laid his hands upon a few sick folk, and healed them.

*And he marvelled because of their UNBELIEF.
And he went round about the villages, teaching.*

– Mark 6:1-6

Jesus went to His own hometown with the plan to bless them and bring God's power to them, just as He had in other cities.

Mark 6:1 tells us that Jesus had just come *"...from thence...."* Where was He just coming from? He had just come from raising Jairus' daughter from the dead. That's a good meeting to be coming from! Jesus is the resurrection and the life, but He had just been in a situation where that resurrection life had raised a little girl from the dead. Going into Nazareth, His own hometown folks could have received that same resurrection power in their lives, but Mark 6:5 tells us that Jesus *"...could there* (in His hometown of Nazareth) *do no mighty work...."* He *couldn't* raise the dead in His own hometown. He certainly went there to do that, if the need arose. He went there to heal and cast out devils, but He *couldn't!* Why? There was a spirit of unbelief that permeated the entire community, and that unbelief caused the Man who could raise the dead to be hindered.

There were people in His hometown who should've been healed, could've been healed, and would've been healed, had they not been surrounded by a community who operated in unbelief.

It can cost you dearly to hang around doubt and unbelief. Protect the spirit of faith in your heart and associate with those of like faith.

An Uncommon Man

Let's look at how the people of Nazareth became a community of unbelievers who missed out on receiving God's power and anointing. If we can see what they did, then we'll know what *not* to do!

Mark 6 tells us that when the people of Nazareth heard Jesus speak, they began questioning, "Where did He get His wisdom from? He's just like us. He's a carpenter with a mama, brothers, and sisters, and we all know them." They tried to pull Him down to their level, treating Him as a common man; but when the anointing is on someone, they're no longer common. They are a carrier of Heaven's power.

Never look at a man under the anointing as being common. Yes, he's a man, but he's a God-touched, God-filled man. Honor what God is doing through him so that you can receive from him. Every man of God has feet of clay; he's got flaws, but we must still honor the anointing and the calling upon his life if we are to benefit from that anointing.

A Life of Honor

When Jesus was in His hometown, the Bible tells us that they were offended at Him.

In Mark, Jesus tells us why they were offended.

> **MARK 6:4**
> **But Jesus, said unto them, A prophet is not without HONOUR, but in his own country, and among his own kin, and in his own house.**

So, Jesus tells us the reason they were offended – they didn't honor Him. Those you honor can never offend you, but those you fail to honor, you can become offended with. Those you honor, you will be able to receive from; those you fail to honor, you won't be able to receive from. What you honor, you will keep; what you fail to honor, you will lose. Dishonor is a poor receiver.

Even if someone acts dishonorably toward you, God still expects you to act honorably toward them. We must never allow our actions to equal the actions of others, but we are to hold the Word of God as our standard. Our actions are to equal God's, and God is honorable to all people at all times, regardless of how they treat Him. To walk in honor toward all men is to keep yourself free from offense. No one you honor can offend you.

Offense will rob from anyone who yields to it, for the offspring of offense is unbelief. Mark 6:5 & 6 tell us that Jesus *"...could there do no mighty work (in His hometown)... And He marvelled because of their UNBELIEF...."*

Unbelief always accompanies offense, and no one yielding to unbelief can receive blessings from God, for God's blessings can only meet faith. Unbelief is a poor receiver of blessings. Offended people are people who are also operating in unbelief. Unbelief is the companion of offense. When you see an offended man, you are also seeing a man who is in unbelief.

Notice the three words in Mark 6:1-6 that show us why the people of Nazareth failed to receive God's power: offense, dishonor, and unbelief. Each of these are deadly to one's spiritual health, and to yield to any one of them is to open yourself up to all three of them.

No one can offend you without your permission. Offense is a decision you make. So make the decision to walk in honor and to never allow offense into your life.

My husband, my mentor, Ed Dufresne, could never have offended me because I always honored him – I made that decision before the opportunity to take offense arose. My spiritual father, Kenneth E. Hagin, could never have offended me. Why? Because I honored him – therefore, offense could not enter in. My pastor could never offend me, for I choose to honor him.

To honor others at all times is to keep yourself free from offense, for honor refuses any opportunity to take offense. To honor all men at all times is a decision to be made *before* the opportunity for offense arises.

Run From Offense

When God places you under a pastor, make a decision to always honor him, and you will safeguard yourself from offense.

The devil wants to get every congregation member offended with their pastor, the staff, or another congregation member so that he can draw them away from their pastor; for the devil knows he can scatter those without a shepherd.

So, his great tactic is to get you out from under the protection of a shepherd.

Never take another man's offense! Offense tries to spread to others. It looks for companionship. It looks for someone else to agree with it. Offense can't stand alone – it seeks to have a crowd gathered around it. A righteous man of faith can stand alone, but not an offended man. Don't borrow another man's offense – protect yourself from it.

Don't allow an offended congregation member or staff member to separate you from your pastor, because they'll forsake you, just like they have forsaken their pastor, and you'll lose out on blessings on account of them.

Remember, your blessing is always connected with another man. Don't leave that man God has connected you with!

Philippians records a prayer Paul prayed for the believers in Philippi.

> **PHILIPPIANS 1:9-11**
> **9 And this I pray, that your love may abound yet more and more in knowledge and in all judgment;**
> **10 That ye may approve things that are excellent; that ye may be sincere and WITHOUT OFFENCE till the day of Christ;**
> **11 Being filled with the fruits of righteousness, which are by Jesus Christ, unto the glory and praise of God.**

It should be quite significant to us that of all the things that can trouble and hinder our fellowship with God and man, offense is the primary one that Paul singled out as being the most devastating. When Paul was led by the Spirit of God to pray that believers would live free from offense, the Spirit of God was warning us of the great harm offense brings to our lives; offense is one of the enemy's main strategies.

Let's look again at Jesus in His hometown of Nazareth. Mark 6:5 & 6 tell us, *"And he* (Jesus) *could there do no mighty work...."* Now, wasn't Jesus the Word made flesh? Yes, He was. So, we could correctly read this same verse as, *"And THE WORD could there do no mighty work...."* Not only that, Jesus was the express image of God. He was the exact representation of God, so we could also correctly read this verse as, *"And GOD could there do no mighty work...."* So, we see the dangerous position that offended people are in – Jesus can't help them, the Word can't help them, and God can't help them. What God wants to bless them with can't reach them. Offense puts a man outside the reach of blessing; blessing can't flow in.

How do you help offended people? In Philippians 1:9-11, Paul instructed us to pray for people to be free from offense. As we do, God will deal with them regarding their offense and bring it to light. They must then repent of that offense and turn their back on it. When they repent for being in offense, then they can once again receive from God.

Offense is dangerous, for Mark 6:6 tells us that Jesus marveled because of the unbelief of those in Nazareth.

Offended people are in unbelief, and faith is weakened in the heart of someone in offense; without faith you can't receive anything from God. How dangerous offense is to our spiritual well-being!

Now we can see more clearly why the Holy Spirit and Paul singled out praying for believers to be free from offense.

How needful it is for us to pray this way for believers today. Let's look again at this prayer Paul prayed, and we will see that we are given in this same passage the cure for offense. *"And this I pray, that your LOVE MAY ABOUND yet more and more in knowledge and in all judgment...."* How can we keep ourselves free from offense? By walking in love. Love is the cure for every flaw of man. When love reigns, failure and weakness become things of the past. If you love someone, you'll honor them, and then offense can't enter in.

Offense is one of the main strategies the devil uses to keep us from receiving what God has provided for us. Offense is also one of the primary tricks the devil uses to draw believers out from under their pastor. But remember, your blessing is always connected with another man of God. Don't leave your man of God out of offense!

Chapter 6

Bible Prosperity Is Linked to Your Divine Connection

In Genesis 13, we read about Abram (God had not yet changed his name to Abraham) and Lot and the tragic mistake Lot made. Abram and Lot had so many cattle that the land couldn't support all the herds, and strife arose between those keeping the herds. Abram came to Lot and said, *"...Let there be no strife, I pray thee, between me and thee, and between my herdman and thy herdman; for we be brethren"* (Gen. 13:8). Abram knew that nothing stops increase like strife.

> **GENESIS 13:9-11**
> **9 Is not the whole land before thee? separate thyself, I pray thee, from me: if thou wilt take the left hand, then I will go to the right; or if thou depart to the right hand, then I will go to the left.**
> **10 And Lot lifted up his eyes, and beheld all the plain of Jordan, that it was well watered every where, before the Lord destroyed Sodom and Gomorrah, even as the garden of the Lord, like the land of Egypt, as thou comest unto Zoar.**
> **11 THEN LOT CHOSE....**

The Amplified Classic translation reads, *"Then Lot chose for himself...."*

When we do the choosing for ourselves, rather than following God's plan for our life, we can be assured that we, like Lot, will end up living outside of the blessings of God.

Abram was a man of faith who lived in fellowship with God. All those connected with his life were blessed by his faith. Others benefited from his life of faith and were the recipients of the rewards of his faith.

Lot was no different. His life was blessed by Abram's faith, and as a result, his prosperity was greatly increased. Remember this: right associations will increase you, but wrong associations will decrease you.

How important it is to have your life connected with a man of God who possesses a strong spirit of faith! Not only are we to have a strong spirit of faith flowing through our beings, but when we are in fellowship with others who possess strong faith, we live under a double blessing – that of our own faith and that which comes from another's faith.

There are believers who never develop their own faith and just live under the blessing of someone else's faith – maybe that of a godly spouse or a godly relative – but without the influence of that loved one's faith, they would struggle, since they didn't develop their own faith.

Yes, we should always keep spiritual company with those of strong faith, but we should never neglect to cause our own faith to be strengthened through meditation on the Word of

God and through being a doer of the Word in every instance of life. To be able to live under the fullness of God's blessings, we must not live totally dependent upon the faith of another, but we must develop our own faith. Don't mistake another man's faith as your own.

In the life of Lot, we see the tremendous blessing, prosperity, and increase he possessed as a result of his connection with Abram. Yet, even in the midst of his great blessing and wealth, he made a crucial mistake – he began thinking that this blessing originated with him. He thought nothing of leaving his companionship with Abram. He forgot that his blessing was connected with another man.

Although at one time Lot's possessions were great, his blessings did not equal Abram's. The Bible tells us that Abram was rich in cattle, silver, and gold (Gen. 13:2). Abram's wealth was threefold, but Lot's wealth was only that of cattle; his prosperity had only reached one-third of what Abram possessed. There was much more he could have possessed if he would have chosen to stay with Abram. When Lot parted from Abram, he began losing and continued losing until he was reduced to nothing. But not so with Abram – Abram only increased, and he continued increasing for the rest of his life.

How different life would have been for Lot had he protected his fellowship and companionship with Abram.

When Abram suggested that they should part company because the land couldn't support their wealth in herds of cattle, Lot should have remembered that his blessing was connected to this man of God. He should have told Abram, "I'm not leaving you! I'll barbeque some of my cattle, because I'd rather give up my cattle than to give up my place with you."

This is the same mistake many believers make. When they first arrive at a church that preaches the Word, many times their lives are in shambles with all kinds of crisis and problems. But as they're faithful to sit under their pastor and to become doers of the Word, their lives start turning around. Where they had once experienced failure and loss, they start to walk in victory and increase; their marriages are restored, their homes have peace, their children begin serving God, their bodies are healed, their finances are blessed, and God's blessing on them becomes apparent.

As they experience blessing, they sometimes forget that the blessing is connected to their pastor, who preached God's Word and faith to them, and connected to their faithfulness to their local church. Little by little, they get pulled away from that church, thinking that the blessing originated with them. But, by and by, something comes along that pulls them away from their local church. They leave with only a small measure of the blessing compared to what they could have had if they would have stayed. Then, because they leave their place of blessing, they, like Lot, begin losing the measure of blessing they did have.

Notice that Abram, being the spiritual father, didn't try to keep Lot near him. It was Lot's job to stay near Abram.

Remember Elisha's response to Elijah on the day he was carried away on the chariot of fire (2 Kings 2). Three times Elijah tried to leave Elisha behind, but Elisha replied, "I'm not leaving you!" And his blessing for staying was that of a double portion of the anointing Elijah had on him. It's the son's job to stay near the father! It's not the man of God's job to keep you close to him – it's your job to stay close to him!

When Lot later moved to the city of Sodom, he became a leader in that city, but we know this – you can't live in the city with herds of cattle. Lot got rid of all of his cattle to live among the godless men of Sodom, but he didn't get rid of even some of his cattle to stay with Abram, the man of God. What loss this wrong decision and wrong priority cost him! It cost him his wife, his children, his wealth – it cost him everything!

Bible Prosperity

As long as Lot stayed in the will of God, he was prosperous. God wants you prosperous. But God doesn't want your prosperity to get in the way of obeying Him and staying in His will.

What does this mean for us today? God will prosper you, but don't start serving your prosperity and letting it get in the way of your obedience to God.

If you're offered a promotion on your job, it may bring financial increase, but what if that job position required you to work on some Sundays and miss some Sunday services at church? Would you allow that job to pull you away from your man of God, your pastor, just to gain financial increase? That's what Lot did, and it cost him.

God isn't going to give you a job that pulls you away from your local church – but the devil will! God isn't going to give you a job that offers you financial increase at the expense of your spiritual life – but the devil will!

Proverbs 10:22 tells us, *"The blessing of the Lord, it maketh rich, and he addeth NO SORROW with it."* When God increases you, it won't cause a different arena of your life to decrease. He won't rob from one arena of your life to supply another arena. He won't give you a job that increases you financially, but decreases you spiritually. Bible prosperity means you don't have to rob from one arena of life in order to supply another arena of life.

No, there's no sorrow with the prosperity God blesses us with. When God prospers us, every arena of our life is increased, enriched, and strengthened.

When God does something, it's good for the whole, not just for a part. On the six days of Creation, after creating a part, God would look at it and say that it was good. But when His Creation was complete, He looked at the whole – how it all looked together – and said that it was *all* good (Gen. 1:31). We can see from this that God's plans benefit everything involved, not just a part. When you make a change in life, is the change good for every arena of your life, or just for one part of your life?

That job promotion might be good for your career, but is it good for your marriage and your children? That move to another city might be good for your business, but will it pull you away from serving in your local church or from the pastor who is your divine connection? If it's not good for every arena of your life, it's not God!

When we live within God's will and plan for our lives, every arena of our life is blessed and flourishes. But when we live according to *our* plans, only a few arenas of our lives may seem to flourish, but not every arena will. Walking in our own plans may bring a measure of increase in some arenas, but there will be sorrow in other arenas that pollutes any increase.

So it was with Lot. When he was living in the will of God, which was under Abram's fellowship, every arena of his life flourished. But when Lot chose for himself, ending up in Sodom, he ended up eventually losing everything: his spiritual connection with Abram, his wife, children, home, social position, wealth, all his possessions, and the morality of his children (for they later committed incest with their father). His own way cost him everything God had previously blessed him with.

What's Your Priority?

In Philippians we see a prayer Paul prayed for those in Philippi.

PHILIPPIANS 1:9
And this I pray, that your love may abound yet more and more in knowledge and in all judgment.

PHILIPPIANS 1:10 (AMPC)
So that you may surely learn to sense what is VITAL, and approve and PRIZE WHAT IS EXCELLENT AND OF REAL VALUE [RECOGNIZING THE HIGHEST AND THE BEST, and distinguishing the moral differences]....

What does this mean? It means that we must learn what should be priority in our lives and keep our priorities in place.

What an important prayer this is for us to pray for believers today. How different believers would live if they always understood what is most vital and important in life and lived with that in view. Believers need to place priority on the proper things.

Lot lost view of what was most important. He held to his possessions at the cost of severing his vital spiritual connection with Abram. Spiritual matters are of greater importance than natural matters.

God wants His children to be blessed with all good things, and He will add all things that we need as we put God's Kingdom first in our lives. But, if necessary, we must be willing to let go of some things so that we may hold to that which is most needful.

Maybe one should postpone having that second car or larger home if they'll have to work longer hours to support it, miss services in their church, do less serving in the church, and be away from their family and children too much. Yes, God wants you prosperous, but not at the sake of neglecting that which is most vital and important. If you will seek first the Kingdom of God and His righteousness, the natural things you need will be *added* to you (Matt. 6:33). God wants you to have the things you want, and as you put your priority on spiritual matters, He will add to you the things you need and want.

If believers will give spiritual matters their proper place in their lives, their spiritual health and faith will flourish, and the blessings of God will become obvious.

Our purpose in life is not to be that of accumulating natural things, but rather, fulfilling His plan for our lives, causing our fellowship with God to be strong and unbroken, being doers of the Word in every arena of life, and being a blessing to humanity. When you make these things your priority, God will bless you with financial and natural blessings.

If you'll hold to the right things and to the most important things in life, then the unimportant and the natural things of life won't get a hold on you.

Lot should have let go of some of his cattle to remain with the man of God, for he would have ended up being a far wealthier man in every arena of life.

There may be seasons in life where we need to cut some things away from our lives if they draw us away from the things of God and away from our fellowship with Him.

Luke 18:18-22 records the sad story of a rich, young ruler who questioned Jesus about what to do to inherit eternal life. Jesus told him, "Keep the commandments."

"Yes, I do that and have done it from my youth," the ruler affirmed.

But Jesus spoke further, *"...Yet lackest thou ONE thing...."* It only takes one thing to destroy many things. It only takes one area of disobedience to lose out on God's best.

How does God prosper us? Matthew 6:33 reads, *"But seek ye first the kingdom of God, and his righteousness; and all these things shall be ADDED unto you."* Who does the "adding"? God does the adding!

What does it mean to *"...seek ye first the kingdom of God..."*? God's Kingdom is a *spiritual* kingdom; it's not a natural kingdom, a business kingdom, or a financial kingdom. So, we must put spiritual things first – not business, financial, or natural things.

If we'll put Kingdom things first – doing that which strengthens our own spiritual life, furthering God's Kingdom here on the earth, and being a blessing to humanity – God will add the good things of life to us. He'll add the pay raise, the job promotion, the larger home, and the second car. But if we try to add to ourselves the pay raise, the job promotion, the larger home, and the second car, we'll end up putting

Kingdom things second or last, instead of first. Our spiritual life will suffer when *we* try to do the adding.

Chapter 7

Protecting Divine Connections

By looking at the story of how Paul and Barnabas' relationship was brought to an end, we can further reinforce the necessity of protecting the divine connections with men of God who are brought into our lives.

Let's look at the incident recorded in Acts.

> **ACTS 15:36-41**
> **36 And some days after Paul said unto Barnabas, Let us go again and visit our brethren in every city where we have preached the word of the Lord, and see how they do.**
> **37 And Barnabas determined to take with them John, whose surname was Mark.**
> **38 But Paul thought not good to take him with them, who departed from them from Pamphylia, and went not with them to the work.**
> **39 And the contention was so sharp between them, that they departed asunder one from the other: and so Barnabas took Mark, and sailed unto Cyprus;**
> **40 And Paul chose Silas, and departed, being recommended by the brethren unto the grace of God.**

41 And he went through Syria and Cilicia, confirming the churches.

When we look at this passage of Scripture, we see that Paul had it in his heart to revisit the churches where they had been previously, to strengthen them and see how they were doing. But we see where the problem begins, *"And Barnabas DETERMINED...."* Anytime someone gets "determined" that something is going to be their way, contention will be the end result.

We see other places in the Bible where Barnabas' determination was a blessing when it was used rightly. When the churches were slow to receive Paul into their fellowship, Barnabas was determined that they would receive Paul. But in this other incident, Barnabas became self-willed in his determination and the outcome was to his great disadvantage.

The Holy Ghost had joined Paul and Barnabas together as a team to accomplish God's work (Acts 13:2), but Barnabas was determined that Mark, his nephew, was going to accompany them on their journey. The divine connection in Barnabas' life was with Paul, not Mark. Mark was his relative, but Paul was his divine connection. Never place a natural connection higher than a divine connection.

Acts 13 introduces us to the divine connection between Paul and Barnabas.

Acts 13:2 & 4
2 As they ministered to the Lord, and fasted, the Holy Ghost said, Separate me Barnabas and

Saul (Paul) **for the work whereunto I have called them.
4 So they** (Barnabas and Paul)**, BEING SENT FORTH BY THE HOLY GHOST, departed....**

Linked by the Holy Ghost

There are no associations in our lives as important as those linked by the Holy Ghost. They are few and far between, but they are the most valuable associations we will ever have. At all costs, guard and protect those associations. Don't assume that the scripture stating, *"...What therefore God hath joined together, let not man put asunder"* (Matt. 19:6) pertains only to a marriage. Any divine connection must be protected!

God will direct every believer where they are to go to church to be pastored. That pastor God directs you to is to be one of those rare, divine associations that is precious in your life. No, it's not in the developing of a relationship with them on a natural level by going to dinner with them or trying to become their buddy, but we receive the most from them in the church services, when they are ministering under the anointing of God.

At all costs, guard those divine associations; never let anything divide you from them. If God is the One who authors a divine association, such as Paul and Barnabas had, then only God can release you from such an association. Don't let offense, self-will, or any other divisive thing enter in.

Barnabas traded off his divine connection just to get his own way. What a sad day it was for Barnabas! Sometimes we think we've won by getting our way – but what a loss he suffered, just to win. Was he really the winner? Unquestionably, no!

Sometimes we may have to give up our own preferences just to stay in the place where God has put us – but we'll never lose by doing what we need to do in order to protect what God has brought into our lives.

Paul didn't have a personal conflict with Mark; Paul was protecting Mark. He knew that since Mark had previously abandoned them when faced with persecution, he was not ready for the persecution they would face in the future. Paul was protecting this young minister; he wasn't against him.

How important it is to protect young ministers by not putting them in positions for which they are not yet developed.

Sometimes, it seems that pastors and those in full-time ministry can create unnecessary hardships by placing someone in a position prematurely. When that happens, the person can end up causing damage or disappointment, and then the leaders are hurt by them. But the leader is primarily to blame for putting them in a position they're not yet equipped for. Even if someone has a call, that certainly doesn't mean they are qualified or prepared to step into it yet.

This is something Paul understood; that's why he was seeking to protect Mark from being placed in a position prematurely.

A Lasting Supply

Sometimes, pastors have such needs in their various departments that they place people in positions before they've been proven or qualified for that place, or they bring someone in from outside their congregation to fill a position. That doesn't always work, for they might not have the pastor's vision implanted in their hearts.

If possible, the best thing is to raise up those from within who have the heart of their pastor, but that can take time. Yes, it may mean that some departments have to wait before they're developed, but slow growth is good growth, it's healthy growth, it's lasting growth. As Dr. Lester Sumrall said, "Weeds grow quickly, but it takes time for flowers to bloom." Give things the proper time needed for them to bloom – including people. Give them time to bloom before placing them in leadership. It takes time to observe someone's faithful, active involvement in a church before you can become properly acquainted with them – to know how they will respond in a variety of different circumstances and in the tests that come in life.

I've seen situations where churches were in such need of musicians that they placed baby Christians, who had a valid music gift, in leadership positions, but they were too young and unskilled in the Word to be placed in those positions. The end result was that the church was harmed and so was the young believer.

As pastors, our job toward our congregation is to *mature* the sheep, not just use their giftings for our own benefit without looking ahead to see how placing these young believers in leadership can damage them. They are then subject to falling prey to thinking of themselves more highly than they ought, and they can then become difficult for anyone to lead and guide.

Paul was protecting Mark from being put in a position that was above his spiritual growth and development.

We are not to just put someone in a position because we need that place filled, but it must also be best for the one filling the position.

Sailing Out of History

When Paul and Barnabas parted company, Paul took Silas with him. Acts 16 tells us what happened to Paul and Silas – they were whipped and thrown in prison. So, we can see what Paul protected the young Mark from. Mark wasn't ready for that kind of persecution, and Paul knew it. How did Paul know it? Because Acts 15:38 tells us that Mark abandoned them when they were in Pamphylia due to persecution.

What happened to Barnabas? Acts 15:39 says, *"...so Barnabas took Mark, and sailed...."* Barnabas not only sailed away with Mark that day, but he sailed off the pages of history that day. We never hear of Barnabas again. As long as he held to his divine connection with Paul, we have record of what God accomplished through him. But the day he sailed away from his divine connection, we lose record of anything else he may have done for God – the Holy Ghost no longer saw fit to record his doings in the Holy Scriptures. What a sad day for Barnabas! He won his way – but what a loss!

Yet, Paul moves forward with God and goes on to pen the majority of the New Testament; so it's easy to see who was right in that situation.

Not only that, but God was able to bring Mark back into a divine connection with Paul, for 2 Timothy 4:11 reads, *"...Take Mark, and bring him with thee: for he is profitable to me for the ministry."* How wonderful! Mark had matured and grown to the place where Paul, the man of God, is asking for him now. This proves, undoubtedly, that Paul had nothing against Mark personally. He had only been protecting him until he was ready for the work God was preparing him for.

We also see that God had prepared someone else to take Barnabas' place – Silas. What a heartbreak to be replaced on an assignment from Heaven. Let us all be reminded that God is looking for obedience and faithfulness to His call; the cost of falling short in obedience and faithfulness is to lose out on God's best and highest. We must all protect divine associations and divine assignments if we are to finish our race.

A Word to Young Ministers

God will bring pastors and spiritual fathers into your life to train and equip you, but you are to stay under their training and watchful eye.

Elisha is one who would not be pulled away prematurely from his spiritual father, and a double portion of the anointing was his reward for not leaving too soon.

I saw many young ministers move out too soon from under the training of my husband's ministry and anointing and miss out on God's best – they struggled and struggled to make it in the ministry, but all that could have been avoided if they hadn't let the zeal for their own ministry pull them away from their preparation time. Being called is no substitute for being prepared.

Kenneth E. Hagin taught us well, saying, "Preparation time is never lost time." Decide to enjoy your preparation and training – it's all part of God's will; so thrive there, bloom there, flourish there, be content there, and don't let your desire for your own ministry pull you away from your preparation time. Get your desire off the future and be faithful today. Tomorrow will take care of itself as you are faithful and obedient to God today.

Chapter 8

Planted in the Local Church

Those that be PLANTED in the house of the Lord shall flourish in the courts of our God.

They shall still bring forth fruit in old age; they shall be fat and flourishing.

— Psalm 92:13 & 14

The New Testament tells us that we, the believers, are the house of God, but the verses above hold a truth that is reflected in Hebrews 10:25 as well: *"Not forsaking the assembling of ourselves together...."* In other words, "Be planted!" Don't neglect church attendance. Those who are planted are those who don't neglect church attendance.

Psalm 92:13 shows us that the ones that are planted are the ones that will flourish. As they age in God, their fruit increases; they are fat with the anointing, and they flourish in the Word and in God's blessings. The fatness of the anointing on their lives prevents any yoke from going around their necks (Isa. 10:27, AMPC). Their latter years will carry fruit and fulness. These are some of the benefits of having a shepherd in our lives and of being faithful to church attendance.

How wonderful for God to give us a pastor to submit to. How safe that is! Although God will place us under a shepherd, it is still our job to submit to him – to *choose* to be planted.

What does it mean to submit to a pastor? One of my favorite definitions of the word "submit" means the willingness to be led.

It's one thing to attend a church, but it's a whole different thing to submit to a pastor, being willing to be led. Some sit in the pew because it's Sunday morning, but those who mature spiritually are the ones who come to church to receive the Word of God from the man of God. They are there to allow the man of God to speak into their lives and to allow the Word of God to strengthen, enlighten, correct, instruct, and mature them.

The attitude of every congregation member must be one of expecting to receive, ready to believe and act on the Word they hear, and looking to make any needed adjustments.

How much a believer matures is up to the individual rather than just up to the pastor. Every believer has a responsibility to allow himself to be taught and instructed.

We can draw some parallels from a school setting. Yes, every teacher is to come to their classroom prepared to teach the students and to present the teaching in such a way that the students can comprehend it. But just as importantly, each student has a responsibility to allow themselves to be taught. If they're unattentive, distracted, passing notes, whispering with their neighbors, neglectful in their homework, not expecting to receive anything out of the instruction, they will do poorly in the class.

Even so, every church member must come to church services with an attitude of expectancy, ready to be persuaded in the Word of God, ready to believe, and expecting to receive what they need.

Hebrews 4:2 tells us, *"...but the word preached did not profit them, not being mixed with faith in them that heard it."* The preachers can preach the Word with a heart full of faith, but the Word must have the hearer's faith attached to it, not just the preacher's faith. How does the hearer attach faith to the Word? By expecting to hear from God, by drawing on the Word being preached, by treating the Word as his own, and by taking it into his heart and doing it in his daily life.

This draws a line between those who are passively sitting by, waiting for God to do something for them, and those who come in faith, provoking God's power toward their situations. Not only are they planted in the local church, but they also are planting the Word of God in their hearts, making the Word their own by doing the Word in every arena of their life.

It's only the Word we're acting on that we've received. If we're not acting on it, we didn't receive it, no matter how well we may be able to quote it. It's the Word *lived* that transforms one's life.

Planted or Potted?

A believer that's *planted* in a local church is faithful to attend. They receive the Word-based sermon as their word from God. They are also a supply to that church by serving faithfully in some capacity in the church, and they give tithes and offerings.

How important it is for us to be planted. Something that's planted can't be moved when the wind starts blowing.

Too many times, Christians move from one church to another, not planting themselves anywhere. They aren't faithful in attendance or faithful to serve. I would have to refer to them as *potted* plants. There is a difference between being planted and being potted; any gardener knows that.

A potted plant is easily moved; anything coming by can move it – winds of adversity, disgruntled believers, offended people, and the list goes on.

The potted plant is unstable, for you never know what location you'll find it in. However, the one who's planted is easy to locate; they don't move from one place to the next. You can depend on them being in the right place.

Potted plants require a lot of special attention that you don't have to give to a tree that's planted. A tree that's planted draws its moisture out of the ground. But because the potted plant has isolated soil, it can't draw moisture from the ground. It has to have special watering – someone has to take the time to seek it out and give it special attention in watering.

Planted in the Local Church

Christians that aren't planted are like potted plants – requiring special care. They seek to receive special watering. But Christians that are planted are low maintenance; they don't look to require special attention from the pastor. They just steadily draw their water supply from the Word in the sermon that's preached. They take in that Word, they do the Word, and their fruit comes forth. They're stable, and their lives aren't rocked and moved by the winds of adversity.

Potted plants also become root-bound. The roots grow for a time, but have no place to go, so they just twist up in the base of the container; then the plant's growth is stunted because there's no more development or depth of root. The pot is a limiter to the plant, not allowing further growth; the plant is, therefore, limited in its growth. Those who aren't planted in a local church will never develop to full maturity – they will be stunted in their growth. They're so isolated that they are only a limited blessing to those around them. Their bad spiritual habits stunt and limit their growth.

Trees that are planted have a root system that is free to spread wide and go deep because there are no limits. The roots reach out and spread wide and deep, causing the strength of the tree to be great when faced with any winds that come. They are free to grow to their full measure.

God tells us that we are to be planted in a local church, for that's the only way we'll ever grow to our full maturity and bear much fruit.

Some believers claim to be part of a local church and to have a pastor, but they don't "dig in" and do their share of the work in the church family. Everyone needs to be planted, receive their supply, and bring their supply to the church family.

Traveling Ministers Need a Pastor

It's also important that traveling ministers and their families be planted in a local church and have a pastor. Oh, yes, their calendar may keep them from being in many of the services or from being a regular worker in a department, but when they are home, they and their family should show themselves to be actively involved and supportive of their pastor.

Paul told young ministers to, *"...be an example..."* (1 Tim. 4:12). How important for all those in the fivefold ministry to be an example to the rest of the Body of Christ and to show themselves to be submitted to a pastor.

Yes, we all need a pastor; we all need someone to speak into our life. I need a pastor! I need his voice in my life. When ministering, I often refer to my pastor. I want our congregation to know of his importance in my life. I want to be an example to the congregation.

We must all give these things their proper place in our lives if we are to live as fully blessed as God desires.

Chapter 9

Perfecting Our Faith

In this chapter, we're going to look at another great benefit of having a shepherd and of being planted in a local church.

Let's look at 1 Thessalonians 3:10. *"Night and day praying exceedingly that we might SEE YOUR FACE, AND MIGHT PERFECT THAT WHICH IS LACKING IN YOUR FAITH."* In this verse, God's Word connects the "perfecting of your faith" to the man of God "seeing your face." This is something that cannot be overlooked if you are to grow to full spiritual maturity.

God's Word links the condition of our faith to the man of God seeing our face. We can readily see that many believers think they have faith problems, when in reality, they have church attendance problems. If believers will plant themselves under a pastor in a local church, come to church services with an expectant, hungry heart, take hold of the Word, and be a doer of that Word, they will have strong faith. But those who are unfaithful to church attendance will not have the kind of robust faith that every believer needs to live victoriously. Neglecting church attendance, as warned against in Hebrews 10:25, will cheat their life and their faith.

The Need for Faith

Before we go any farther, let's look at the need for faith in our lives. The subject of faith is one of the most important messages in the Bible. Let's consider for a moment the importance faith has and how it affects every facet of our lives.

Ephesians 2:8 says, *"For by grace are ye saved through faith...."* So, we see that it takes faith to even be born again.

In Romans 14:23, we read, *"...whatsoever is not of faith is sin."* Every action that reaches God and blesses humanity must have faith attached to it.

In 2 Corinthians 5:7 we read, *"For we walk by faith, not by sight."* Our manner of life is to be that of faith. Faith is to be evident in every action we make.

Hebrews 11:6 tells us, *"But without faith it is impossible to please him...."* For God to be pleased, faith must be active, for then He can work on our behalf. It doesn't please Him when He can't work on our behalf, because He so longs to. We can also read this same scripture as follows, *"Without faith it is impossible...."* Faith is what makes the impossible possible.

First John 5:4 tells us, *"...this is the victory that overcometh the world, even our faith."* For us to walk in the victory that is ours, faith must be active. Our victory is waiting for our faith to show up.

Jesus stated, *"...According to your faith be it unto you"* (Matt. 9:29). We receive in life according to our faith.

We can see from all of these scriptures that faith is one of the most important messages in God's Word; faith is essential for us to receive salvation and victory and for the impossible to be made possible.

Every believer has faith. *"...God hath dealt to every man the* (same) *measure of faith"* (Rom. 12:3). God deposits the beginning measure of faith into the spirit of every born-again believer (2 Cor. 4:13). It is then up to each believer to cause that faith to grow and be active as it's fed on the Word and acted on. Second Thessalonians 1:3 reads, *"...your faith GROWETH exceedingly...."* God expects us to cause the measure of faith He gave us to grow.

The Prophet "Sees" David

One way your faith is perfected is by being in the local church where the pastor can "see your face."

As grateful as we are for good Bible-teaching books and materials, they will never take the place of a pastor in your life; they will never replace the man of God "seeing your face."

In 1 Samuel 16, we read the story of when God spoke to Samuel to go and anoint one of the sons of Jesse to be king. One by one, Jesse's sons stood before the prophet. "Is this the one?" the prophet would ask God. As the first son passed before Samuel, he thought to himself, *Surely this eldest son would be the one God has chosen. He's so stately in stature. He has the look of a king.*

But God answered the prophet, "No, he is not the one. I have refused him." Since he was refused, it gives us the idea that God considered him.

Every son of Jesse stood before the prophet, and as each one stood before the prophet's face, the word of knowledge, which is a gift of the Spirit, would operate through the prophet to let him know whether this son was God's choice. It wasn't until David was finally brought before the man of God that the word came to him, "This is the one!"

There's something we can learn about the operation of the gifts of the Spirit by looking at this event. When the man of God saw each one's face, the gifts of the Spirit went into operation. God didn't tell Samuel that David was God's choice until he saw David's face.

Now this gives us some insight into why Paul longed to "see the face" of those he was writing to.

The Gifts of the Spirit

As the Spirit wills, the gifts of the Spirit can go into operation – primarily, when a man of God sees someone face to face.

In pastoring, when I saw the face of one in our congregation who was going through a test or trial, God would sometimes give me a word of knowledge or a word of wisdom to help them, as the Spirit willed. But that didn't happen until I saw their face.

There was one particular occasion in which this happened. As I was walking through our sanctuary prior to a service, I passed by one of the young ladies who was a faithful member of the church. As I walked past her, I had a word of knowledge about a test she was facing and I knew the answer for her.

For a period of about two weeks, every time I would walk past her, the same thing would come to me. So, after the service one evening, I called her into the side room. I didn't tell her all that the Spirit of God told me, for I didn't want to embarrass her. I didn't even tell her God had told me anything. I just began the conversation by saying, "Several years ago I faced a particular test and this is what I did to gain victory over that test." I told her of a personal trial I went through that related to her test, and I proceeded to instruct her on how I stood on the Word of God to walk out of that victoriously.

As I talked, I saw light come to her face. She saw what I was telling her; she made the connection. For the previous two weeks, she had walked around with a cloud over her head, but now, the light came and the cloud left.

Later that week, I saw her at another church service and she pulled me aside. "Pastor Nancy, I did what you said you did in your test, and I want you to know that it worked for me. That battle in my mind has stopped. I'm free from the torment I was in."

Now, just think, I was able to reach her with the help of the Holy Spirit because of one reason – I was able to see her face. God didn't tell me how to help her when I was at home; He didn't give me her answer until I saw her face. That's not to say that God can't tell you about someone unless you see them, but if a gift of the Spirit is needed to help someone, it will primarily operate when you see their face.

I've noticed that when I get within close proximity to someone, sometimes a gift of the Spirit will go into operation, as the Spirit wills, and He will speak to me about them. That's what happened to Samuel with Jesse's sons. As they stood in front of the prophet, the Spirit spoke to him.

How needful it is for your pastor to see your face. Few people have ever seen Jesus, but God does give us a pastor's face to see, and he is the under-shepherd of the Great Shepherd.

There were times when I had a sermon prepared to teach, but when I walked out and saw the look of despair on the face of a particular person who was going through a test or trial, God changed my sermon to minister on faith so that their faith would be encouraged.

A man of God is anointed to see your face and to be able to feed into your life the help you need.

No, God doesn't tell pastors things about people's lives so they can tell people, "I know what you've been doing!" No – God tells pastors and other ministers these things so that people can be helped. When God tells me some of these things, I don't share them with anyone except that person; and again, it's only so they can be helped. God doesn't tell a pastor everything about everyone, but as the Spirit wills, He will tell that which will help and protect.

Addressing Difficult Situations

There were times the Spirit of God warned me about a church visitor whose motives and intentions weren't right; an alarm went off in my spirit. I didn't just sit around and wait for them to cause a problem or difficulty in the sheepfold. I called them aside privately and politely told them the importance of being under the right pastor so that they could receive God's supply into their life, but that I wasn't that pastor. I wasn't the one who was to be that supply for them. I let them know it would be a waste of their time to attend our church for a year or two, only to later realize that they were in the wrong place. By handling the situation this way, I was able to save myself and other congregation members from a lot of potential difficulty.

As pastors, we don't have to receive just anybody into our sheepfold when the Spirit warns us about them. As a parent, I don't allow just anyone into our home. Why would it be any different in the church home?

If the Spirit reveals to me that someone would bring difficulty in the church, I honor the Spirit of God by giving heed to His warning. To do nothing and to just let difficulties arise that harm others in the church would dishonor the Holy Spirit and grieve Him.

It must be understood that I dealt with situations like that only when I had that alarm in my spirit.

Then, there were times when a person I had never seen before walked into our church, and the Spirit of God warned me, "Watch that person." Why would God tell me that? To protect the other sheep.

Sometimes in meeting people, I would sense a "check" on the inside of me about them. I just knew that there was something not right about them; I knew that they allowed things in their lives that weren't pleasing to the Lord. God would direct them to the church to allow them to sit under the Word and give them an opportunity to let the Word change their lives, if they would become doers of the Word.

While that process was going on in their lives, they weren't allowed to serve in any capacity of the helps ministry. But as they proved themselves, they were slowly introduced into serving in some capacity where they weren't working closely with other congregation members.

However, if they didn't allow the Word to do a work in their life, that same Word caused them to eventually leave because they became offended at the Word they refused to receive.

In pastoring, God equipped me with the gifts needed to keep the sheepfold safe.

Naturally, I'm not a confrontational person, but I had to learn to appropriately confront those who would injure or jeopardize the church family. If I hadn't, then I would be accountable for any damage done against the congregation. Some pastors may think they are operating in mercy to not confront what should be confronted, but mercy or walking in love does not mean being permissive to wrong doing. We must do what is right to protect the sheep. That's the shepherd's job.

Pastors must be sensitive to the Holy Spirit and expect Him to guide them in every area affecting the church, for He will always lead us right, but we must take time to hear Him and obey His leadings.

Hebrews 13:17 instructs us to, *"Obey them that have the rule over you, and submit yourselves: for they watch for your souls, AS THEY THAT MUST GIVE ACCOUNT...."* Every shepherd will stand before God and give an account for the sheep that are placed under his care. But how can God expect the shepherd to answer for the sheep if God doesn't let the shepherd know some things about the sheep? Since shepherds will give an account for the sheep, then shepherds have a right to expect God to speak to them about the sheep under their care.

God doesn't tell shepherds everything about all the sheep, but He will tell them what they need to know to better help, instruct, and protect them.

For example, if a church member is having difficulty receiving their healing, a pastor could rightly make a request of God saying, "Father, since I'm going to have to give an account for their soul, I ask You to show me how I can better help them. I've laid hands on them and taught them Your Word, yet they have failed to receive their healing. I'm asking you to show me where we're missing it." Time and time again, God caused me to know where people in our congregation were missing it so I could help them. Since I was their shepherd and must give an account of them, God was always faithful to speak to me regarding the condition of the sheep under my care.

Don't Float

For those who float from church to church, submitting themselves to no pastor, what pastor could pray like that for them? What shepherd are they under? Who would God speak to about them? When someone doesn't have a shepherd, they don't have anyone watching over their soul. There's not that pastoral protection over the one who isn't submitted to a pastor.

We had a precious member of our congregation, who has since gone home to be with the Lord, who traveled and sang with Aimee Semple McPherson. She also attended Mrs. McPherson's Bible school. She told us how Sister Aimee often warned her congregation and the Bible school students, "Don't be church tramps, traveling from one church to another." What a valid word of caution that is! Be where God tells you to be and be faithful.

We need to learn to "connect the dots." When we're where God tells us to be, we flourish. When we're not, we face difficulties that could have been avoided.

A Crippled Man Healed

How needful it is for the pastor to see the face of his sheep. Let's look at another passage in the Bible that further illustrates this truth.

> **ACTS 14:8 & 9**
> **8 And there sat a certain man at Lystra, impotent in his feet, being a cripple from his mother's womb, who never had walked:**
> **9 The same heard Paul speak: who** (Paul) **STEADFASTLY BEHOLDING HIM** (the crippled man)**, AND PERCEIVING....**

Notice again, the man of God is seeing the crippled man's face, and when he does, he perceives something.

What is it that Paul perceives? *"...Perceiving that he had faith to be healed."* Paul sees his face and perceives that there's faith in the man's heart to be healed. But is the man healed? No! It's important to see something here. People can have the faith to be healed, yet not receive their healing. What's the problem? The man has *imperfect* faith.

Remember what 1 Thessalonians 3:10 says: *"...that we might see your face, and might PERFECT that which is lacking in your faith."*

If the man has faith to be healed, why isn't he healed? Because he has *imperfect* faith. How do we know his faith is imperfect? Because if his faith was perfect, he would have had perfect health. But because this crippled man is at the right place – the place where the man of God is able to see his face – his faith is about to be made perfect, just like we read about in 1 Thessalonians 3:10.

In Acts 14:10, Paul gives the crippled man the answer that will help his faith to be perfected. *"(Paul) said with a loud voice, Stand upright on thy feet...."* How was the man's faith imperfect? He had the faith to be healed, but perfect faith will act! The man was lacking action – he needed to put an action with the faith he possessed.

How Faith Works

Remember this, faith *comes* by hearing (Rom. 10:17), but faith doesn't *operate* by hearing – faith operates or is released by *speaking* or by *acting* in line with the Word.

Faith is in the spirit of the believer, but faith must be released out of their spirit before it will ever benefit them. How is that faith released? Through words and actions that are in line with God's Word.

When you hear the Word, you believe; but when you speak or act on the Word, you receive!

Romans 10:10 tells us, *"For with the heart man believeth unto righteousness; and with the MOUTH CONFESSION is made unto salvation."*

This crippled man heard the word preached and believed, but the faith he had wasn't released because of his lack of action. But because he was around a man of God who understood how faith operated, Paul was able to help him perfect his faith by telling him what he lacked – action.

Look at what happened when the crippled man did what Paul said, *"...And he leaped and walked"* (Acts 14:10). If the crippled man had not been sitting under a man who understood how to put action to faith, he would have failed to receive his miracle.

What kind of man of God should you be sitting under? One who lives a life of faith, one who teaches you about faith, one who can help you to perfect your faith!

Too many times, believers stay home when they hit a test or trial; they stay home when they don't feel good. No! Get to church! Let the man of God see your face! He's anointed to see your face and help you perfect your faith so you can receive your help!

No, he doesn't have to lay hands on you or call you out specifically with a word from God. He doesn't even have to know about the test you're going through. But when he's preaching or teaching under the anointing, you can make a demand on God and say to yourself, "I'm expecting to receive the help I need, so I'm taking the Word my pastor is teaching, and I'm making it my own." You can come to church like that, expecting God to speak to you, and you'll receive what you need! That's called faith, and it pleases God. God answers faith!

Look at what Paul wrote:

> **1 THESSALONIANS 2:8**
> **So being affectionately desirous of you, we were willing to have IMPARTED UNTO YOU, not the gospel of God only, but ALSO OUR OWN SOULS, because ye were dear unto us.**

Thank God for the Word that your pastor teaches you, but when you're in the midst of a test, you can receive an impartation from his soul, too. What's in his soul? The anointing and the life of God that permeates his being, his own experience of walking with God, and his own knowledge of the Word.

That's why it's important that we sit under the pastor that God sends us to, so that we can be receiving the right things from his being into ours.

Church – Your Priority

Many in the Body of Christ attend the church that's the most convenient to drive to, the church where the kids' friends go, or the church they grew up in. You need to go to the church where God told you to go. God's not concerned about convenience. He doesn't tell you to go to a particular church just because it's convenient for you. He wants you to go to a church where the pastor feeds you His Word and you are receiving the right kind of impartations.

I would say that approximately 70% of those in our congregation moved from great distances just to be part of our church. They relocated their families just so they could attend church where God told them to be.

Many in the world would scoff at something like that, yet they wouldn't think anything about uprooting their whole family and moving them to the other side of the United States just to take a job promotion.

What about taking a spiritual promotion? Spiritual truths are of far greater value than natural things. Isn't your spiritual well-being worth making whatever move is necessary to be under the pastor God directs you to?

There are also believers who leave their church and move out of town to take a job promotion without even considering if there's a good Word-teaching church in that area. If there's no good church in that area, then that location's not good for you.

People's priorities are going to have to be in order if they are going to live in the victory God has provided for them. Put spiritual things first!

At all costs, get where God told you to be and stay there until He says different.

Don't let finances be your deciding factor. Follow what God says – not finances. If you'll obey God, there will be provision in the place where He told you to be.

Impartations

Let's look at another Scripture along the same lines. It's found in Romans 1:11, *"For I long TO SEE YOU, that I may impart unto you some spiritual gift, to the end ye may be established."* Here again, Paul states the need to "see" them for them to receive more of what God has to impart into them. Impartations help us be established and fulfill what we are called to. They help us in this race we are running.

Although Paul wrote letters to the churches, he let them know that his letters alone weren't enough to impart into them all that God had for them – he had to "see" them for that to happen.

We must have God's Word, but we also need the impartations God has to deposit in us through the ministry gifts He gave the Church: the apostle, prophet, pastor, teacher, and evangelist (Eph. 4:11 & 12). However, they must "see" our faces for these impartations to take place.

In John Wesley's Bible Commentary on Romans 1:11, he stated that these impartations could come through the laying on of hands, through the preaching and teaching of God's Word, and through conversation.

Some of the times of greatest impartations have come to me when sitting around a dinner table with some of God's leaders in the Body of Christ and listening to them talk about God's Word and their experiences. What a treasure of instructions and impartations I have received during those times that enhanced my anointing and ministry!

Chapter 10

Keeping a Right Spirit

First Timothy 3 is a chapter that gives a list of what qualifies a man to stand before the congregation as a minister, but we could also say that it is a list of what disqualifies a man from fulfilling his ministry.

If you'll read 1 Timothy 3 carefully, you'll see that the things listed deal with a man's life *outside* the pulpit – not *in* the pulpit. Many mistakenly think that a minister's success lies primarily with his ministering abilities, but according to the Word of God, his success as a minister is seen primarily in his life outside the pulpit.

There are those sad occasions when a minister's personal life causes him to be brought into question before the people. What is a congregation member to do in a case like that? Well, thank God, the Bible gives us our answer when faced with these kinds of difficulties.

When we look at the lives of King Saul and David (1 Sam. 18-31), we see that King Saul became jealous of David, who lived in the king's palace. Many times the king sought to kill David, but David never raised his hand against him.

When David feared for his life, he fled from the palace of King Saul, but notice how he fled – he fled alone and with his mouth closed!

If situations arise with leadership that cause you to be unable to stay in a local church, there is a right way to leave – leave *alone* and with your mouth closed.

David could have, no doubt, told others in the king's service how the king was mistreating him, and he could have gained their sympathy, but David didn't do that. He didn't seek to turn the king's associates against him.

It is never our job to spotlight the faults and failures of those in leadership. Why is that? David answers that for us in 1 Samuel.

> **1 SAMUEL 24:6**
> **And he said unto his men, The Lord forbid that I should do this thing unto my master, the Lord's anointed, to stretch forth mine hand against him, seeing he is the anointed of the Lord.**

Even though King Saul was yielding to an evil spirit, David still honored the fact that the Lord had anointed him.

This is why we never come against or speak against anyone who we think to be in error – for they are the Lord's anointed. Leave all men in God's hands and never touch someone in word or deed whom the Lord has anointed.

Many Christians would wrongly assume that if a minister is in error or sin that they would have a right to address it. But, again, we must go to God's Word to find our answer.

Moses, who was a pastor to millions of Hebrews, was operating by a bad system. All day long he would sit before the people to judge their differences and solve their conflicts. It isn't humanly possible to single-handedly solve the conflicts of millions of people. After a while, he would have broken his body and mind down from the sheer weight of the task. Moses' system was all wrong to be an effective leader of such a vast congregation. Even though Moses was wrong in the way he was handling this great congregation of people, God never used even *one* of those millions to correct Moses, their leader.

Exodus 18 tells us that Jethro, who was Moses' father-in-law, the priest of Midian, came to visit Moses and saw his error of operating. Jethro then told him how to correct his problem, and the solution proved to be a great blessing.

Who did God use? Jethro, a man of equal anointing. Actually, Jethro was Moses' spiritual father, for Moses lived with and served Jethro for 40 years in the desert after he fled from Egypt. Jethro was the priest of Midian for many years; he was a spiritual leader.

Notice that God didn't use someone of a lesser anointing to correct someone of a higher anointing. That's why God will never tell a congregation member or a staff member to correct a pastor. Sheep don't correct shepherds. God will always use someone of equal or higher anointing to correct those in leadership.

It is the privilege of the sheep to pray for their pastor, but it's never their job to correct their pastor or to confront him. God will handle His man, and He knows who to send to him to bring any needed correction, but it will never be the sheep or the staff.

The pastor has a great responsibility to be an example to the flock of God, but if they fail to be that example, God will deal with them. No congregation member need ever be deceived into thinking they are God's corrective tool. God knows how to deal with His man.

Remember, every man of God has feet of clay – he is human, and he won't be perfect. Be faithful to pray for him and give God time to develop His man.

If a situation calls for you to leave your local church, do so in a way that allows God to bless you. Leave with a closed mouth and leave alone – not taking others with you.

How important it is to maintain a right spirit in difficult situations; but the best way to do that is with a closed mouth, then God's blessings can remain strong upon you.

Those in leadership need our prayers. This is not only a responsibility that every congregation has, but greater than that, it's a privilege to pray for those God has anointed to be leaders.

In Closing

Honoring Your Office

Through over 30 years of ministry, I have seen how important it is for all fivefold ministers to publicly and privately speak well of the pastoral office and to always do that which will bless the local churches. All fivefold ministers must be an example to the sheep in honoring the pastoral office, since it is the office most needed by the sheep. The pastor is the most needed office in the Body of Christ because they live with the sheep day in and day out, and the welfare of the sheep is so dependent upon that office. It's so important that every believer understands the pastor's role in their life.

I've had pastors ask me if I taught these messages in our own local church, and my answer is, "Absolutely!" I'm not teaching about me; I'm teaching about an office I stood in. Paul stated in Romans 11:13, *"...I magnify mine OFFICE."* This honorable office, like all of the fivefold offices, has been given as a gift to the Body of Christ to bring them to their full maturity in Christ. It was my responsibility as the pastor to teach them the pastor's role in that maturing process and in their Christian walk.

My parents were the ones who taught me and my siblings the proper way to respond to them and how to receive from them. They never brought the neighbor in to teach us that – they taught us. If we were behaving dishonorably toward them – *they* dealt with us! They didn't ask the neighbor to come teach us. Likewise, the pastor has the responsibility to train his own sheep about the role of the pastor in their lives and to bring them into a place of honoring that pastoral office, as well as all of the fivefold offices.

Many sheep don't know about or understand the need and importance of having a pastor and of being planted in a local church, but their spiritual, mental, physical, and financial well-being depends upon it. They must be told, they must be taught, for God is bringing the Body of Christ into maturity. Jesus declared, *"...I will build my church; and the gates of hell shall not prevail against it"* (Matt. 16:18).

We are all part of that Church He is building, and it is the victorious Church!

Prayer of Salvation

Heavenly Father, I come to You in the Name of Jesus. Your Word says, *"...him that cometh to me I will in no wise cast out"* (John 6:37). So I know You won't cast me out, but You will take me in, and I thank You for it.

You said in Your Word, *"...If thou shalt confess with thy mouth the Lord Jesus, and shalt believe in thine heart that God hath raised him from the dead, thou shalt be saved. For whosoever shall call upon the name of the Lord shall be saved"* (Rom. 10:9 & 13).

I believe in my heart that Jesus Christ is the Son of God. I believe Jesus died for my sins and was raised from the dead so I can be in right-standing with God. I am calling upon His Name, the Name of Jesus, so I know, Father, that You save me now.

Your Word says, *"...with the heart man believeth unto righteousness; and with the mouth confession is made unto salvation"* (Rom. 10:10). I do believe with my heart, and I confess Jesus now as my Lord. Therefore, I am saved! Thank You, Father.

Please write us and let us know that you have just been born again. When you write, ask to receive our salvation booklets.

To contact us, please email us at
dm@dufresneministries.org
or write to:
Dufresne Ministries
P.O. Box 1010
Murrieta, CA 92564

How To Be Filled With the Holy Spirit

Acts 2:38 reads, *"...Repent, and be baptized every one of you in the name of Jesus Christ for the remission of sins, and ye shall receive the GIFT of the Holy Ghost."* The Holy Ghost is a gift that belongs to each one of God's people. Jesus is the gift God gave the whole world, but the Holy Spirit is a gift that belongs only to God's people.

Jesus told His disciples, *"But ye shall receive POWER, after that the Holy Ghost is come upon you: and ye shall be witnesses unto me..."* (Acts 1:8). When you're baptized with the Holy Spirit, you receive supernatural power that enables you to live victoriously.

Indwelling vs. Infilling

When you're born again, you receive the indwelling of the Person of the Holy Spirit. Romans 8:16 tells us, *"The Spirit itself* (Himself) *beareth witness with our spirit, that we are the children of God."* When you're born again, you know it because the Spirit bears witness with your spirit that you are a child of God; He confirms it to you. He's able to bear witness with your spirit because He's in you; you are *indwelt* by the Spirit of God.

But the Word of God speaks of another experience subsequent to the new birth that belongs to every believer, and that is to be baptized with the Holy Spirit, or to receive the *infilling* of the Holy Spirit.

God wants you to be full and overflowing with the Spirit. Being filled with the Spirit is likened to being full of water. Just because you had one drink of water doesn't mean you're full of water. At the new birth, you received the indwelling of the Spirit – a drink of water. But now God wants you to be filled to overflowing – be filled with His Spirit, baptized with the Holy Ghost.

> **ACTS 2:1-4**
> **1 And when the day of Pentecost was fully come, they were all with one accord in one place.**
> **2 And suddenly there came a sound from heaven as of a rushing mighty wind, and it filled all the house where they were sitting.**
> **3 And there appeared unto them cloven tongues like as of fire, and it sat upon each of them.**
> **4 And they were all FILLED with the Holy Ghost, and BEGAN TO SPEAK WITH OTHER TONGUES, as the Spirit gave them utterance.**

When these disciples were filled with the Holy Ghost, they began to speak with other tongues as the Spirit gave them utterance; they spoke in a language unknown to them. Today, when a believer is filled with the Holy Ghost, they will speak with other tongues too. These are not words that come from the mind of man, but they are words given by the Holy

Spirit; these words float up from their spirit within, and the person then speaks those out.

What is the benefit of being filled with the Holy Ghost with the evidence of speaking in other tongues? First Corinthians 14:2 reads, *"For he that speaketh in an unknown tongue speaketh not unto men, but unto God...."* When you're speaking in other tongues, you're speaking to God – it is a divine means of communicating with your Heavenly Father. This is one of many great benefits.

> **MATTHEW 7:7-11**
> 7 Ask, and it shall be given you...
> 8 FOR EVERY ONE THAT ASKETH RECEIVETH...
> 9 ...what man is there of you, whom if his son ask bread, will he give him a stone?
> 10 Or if he ask a fish, will he give him a serpent?
> 11 If ye then, being evil, know how to give good gifts unto your children, HOW MUCH MORE SHALL YOUR FATHER WHICH IS IN HEAVEN GIVE GOOD THINGS TO THEM THAT ASK HIM?

In this passage, Jesus is saying that when you ask God for something, you shall receive it! Believe that He will give you that which you ask for. When you ask God for something good, He won't give you something that will harm you; He will give you the good thing you ask for. The baptism of the Holy Spirit is a good gift, and when you ask God to fill you with the Holy Spirit, you won't receive a wrong spirit; you will receive this good gift, the gift of the Holy Spirit.

Once you receive the gift of the Holy Ghost, you can yield to this gift any time, speaking in other tongues as often as you choose; you don't have to wait for God to move on you. The more you speak in other tongues, the more you will benefit from this gift. By continuing to speak in other tongues on a daily basis, you will be able to maintain a Spirit-filled life; you will live full of the Spirit.

The more you take time to speak in other tongues, the deeper you'll move into the things of God.

(For more teaching on being filled with the Holy Spirit, I recommend the mini-book, *Why Tongues?* by Kenneth E. Hagin.)

Prayer To Receive the Holy Spirit

"Father, I see that the gift of the Holy Spirit belongs to Your children. So, I come to You to receive this gift. I received my salvation by faith, so I receive the gift of the Holy Spirit by faith. I believe I receive the Holy Spirit now! Since I'm filled with the Holy Spirit now, I expect to speak in other tongues as the Spirit gives me utterance, just like those in Acts 2 on the Day of Pentecost. Thank You for filling me with the Holy Ghost."

Now, words that the Spirit of God gives you will float up from your spirit. You are the one who must open your mouth and speak those words out. The words will not come to your mind, but they will float up from your spirit. Speak those out freely.